To
The Children
of
Calcutta.

On Cruelty.

By the Hon. Secretary,
Calcutta Society for the Prevention
of Cruelty to Animals.

CALCUTTA:
THACKER, SPINK AND CO.

In the interest of creating a more extensive selection of rare historical book reprints, we have chosen to reproduce this title even though it may possibly have occasional imperfections such as missing and blurred pages, missing text, poor pictures, markings, dark backgrounds and other reproduction issues beyond our control. Because this work is culturally important, we have made it available as a part of our commitment to protecting, preserving and promoting the world's literature. Thank you for your understanding.

TO THE CHILDREN OF CALCUTTA.
ABOUT CRUELTY.

"Once upon a time" (for that's the way all old stories begin) there was said to be a band of valiant gentlemen called "Knights errant," who roved about different countries seeking to do deeds of great bravery by releasing captive princesses and knights who were lying chained in castle dungeons belonging to some dreadful giants that I dare say you have read about. These giants were said to be very strong, and very brutal; and that is what many people are that are strong and very ignorant, and so they had pleasure only in cruelty; whilst many (so the stories said) were cannibals, and kept their poor prisoners only to kill and to eat them!

Well, by-and-bye, people began to get very learned, and to *read* and to *think* very much, and so young people began to find that these wonderful stories were all, as you may say, "*joet moot.*" Still, though they were not true, they were not thought to be altogether false, as you shall see; nor altogether useless, because they gave young minds—boys in particular—a love of courage and adventure, and a generous desire to defend the weak and helpless against the strong and the wicked. So these stories became something like fables, in which, as you know, animals of all kinds are made to teach very good and pretty lessons in real life, in a very amusing way; and sure enough, when many boys who had read these stories, and were of noble minds, grew up to be men, they discovered, on looking abroad, that there was a world and all of *real* Knights, *real* work to do, and no "*joot moot.*" They found there were hundreds of cruel giants to do battle with, and thousands of their poor captives to rescue from chains and dungeons and misery more horrible than the old stories ever told of, or I can describe to you. These poor captives,—men, women, and children,—were inhabitants of Africa, called negroes, who, because they were poor, helpless, and unable to defend themselves, were seized by wicked, selfish men—sometimes their own chiefs, or men of another tribe, and sometimes by Europeans. I am sure you will say these were the real "giants" of those days, for they tore them away from fathers and mothers, and sold them by hundreds for money to other giants more cruel than themselves, who chained them together, branded them with red hot irons, and thrust them down into the "holds" of ships. There, with very little air or light, they were tightly packed together, much more cruelly even than you see sheep crammed in pens, or fowls in baskets. In this way they were kept for many days, sometimes hardly getting water to drink, and so carried away across the seas to another country. Many were suffocated to death. In one ship in a storm, when they were shut in altogether, seven hundred died in that dreadful way, and were thrown overboard, and the remainder on reaching the land, were sold for slaves, and made to work very hard without any pay, only for their food!—and as a great poet said—

" ————If they dared complain
Were lashed and tortured until tame again."

I am certain you will feel terribly angry and disgusted at the thoughts of such horrid cruelty and cowardly oppression as this, and perhaps hardly believe it to be true. But it is *quite* true, and so a great many English gentlemen, real knights and nobles, rose up and fought a very hard battle for these poor captives. But they didn't fight in steel armour, with swords, and spears, and guns, though they would have done so if that had been the proper way of fighting;—but they fought with much better weapons, that were sharper than any sword, and yet shed no blood. These were only the words of their mouths; for these knights were very, very clever, and very learned and good, and their words dealt blows on men's hearts that knocked harder than cannon balls upon castle walls, because they were words taught them by God. They showed everybody that selling their fellow creatures, or letting other people do so, if they could prevent it, was most wicked, and made them ashamed of it. Many people wouldn't even buy sugar that came from the West Indies, because it was made by slaves.

So the King of England, with his Knights and councillors, determined there should be no more slavery in his dominions. Then a grand law was made forbidding any more slavery in any country belonging to England, and the King sent out ships of war, and they captured all the slave-holders' vessels that were found at sea taking slaves to English places; released the poor delighted negroes, and burnt their prison ships.

Now this took a very long time and great fighting and patience, and cost a terrible load of money,—more than Two Hundred millions of rupees which the people of England had to pay!—But they did'nt mind that. They were determined there should be no more cruel slavery in any country belonging to Britain. This money, I should tell you, was given to the slave-holders in exchange for their slaves, whom they had bought with money perhaps long before; because you know it was proper to be *just* to the master as well as the slave.

Well, after this, nearly all the other countries of Europe promised to have no more slavery; but I'm sorry to say they have not all kept their promise, though we hope they will do by-and-bye. So there is enough of work yet for some good knights to do in those countries.

Now, you will think that all the giants in Britain were surely killed by this time. No! I'm sorry to say they were not; for, the more people came to understand who the real giants were, the more they discovered in the world, and thousands of people were found serving them, though I must say they didn't seem to know it, and thousands don't know it even to this day! But these giants I am now going to tell you about, who delight in a kind of cruelty which was never even thought about before, are found everywhere—in every city and town, and even little villages—not in Africa or Asia only, but, as I've said, in England itself. Well, here was fresh work for the real knights to do—and plenty of it—for as I've told you, these cruel giants seem to have servants by thousands in all directions, and the poor captive slaves (for here was slavery again) could be counted by hundreds of thousands, and they were treated with shameful cruelty in all sorts of ways. They were beaten—flogged—goaded with sharp spikes—kicked—wounded—half starved—worked till they sometimes dropped—tortured—and abused in many ways, you shall hear more about by-and-bye, and at last most of them put to death in a cruel manner! Now, I may tell you there is no law against their being made slaves, or I ought to say servants, because we believe God who made them intended they should be so, but he intended they should be treated very kindly,—for as another great poet says about them—

"The dear God who loveth us
He made and loveth all."

They were given *in trust*, to be taken care of, and you may depend upon it that God will call to a terrible account all who break that trust after they have once been told about it.

Now, what made all this cruelty the more strange and the more wicked was that these poor creatures were all willing servants, giving all kinds of help to their masters without a murmur, and wanting no other pay in the world than food and a little kindness. Without their help, men could not plough the ground, to sow seed; nor get bread to eat; nor carry merchandize or loads about the country; nor ride in carriages; nor enjoy a thousand pleasures and benefits for which they have to thank these poor willing servants. But what will you think of this cruelty to them when I tell you one thing more—*They were all dumb.*

Certainly you will say, the good knights would put on their swords this time, and hasten to slay these cruel giants and all their servants. No! they had to do just what the others did. And here I may tell you an old story intended to show that mere bravery won't kill giants.

In an island called Rhodes, in the Mediterranean Sea, there was said to be living a giant of another kind—a monstrous dragon, roaming all about the country, killing the people, and eating up all their cattle and flocks. Well, there was a band of knights in that country too, called "Knights of the Cross," and some of them determined to go and kill this dragon. So, about a dozen of them, very strong and brave, all in armour and with swords and spears, rode away, and without knowing anything of the beast they were going to fight, they attacked him at once; but their horses took fright, and in a few minutes some were killed, others thrown down and crushed, and the rest had to run away! So, you see, mere bravery and strength could not kill the giant in this case. Somebody can tell you, another time, something more of what these knights for a long time tried very hard to do by mere bravery, but never could do. Now, amongst this band of soldiers was a clever and good young knight, who determined to try what *he* could do to kill the dragon. So, he first rode off to the place where the beast had been seen, and examined it very carefully at a distance whilst it was asleep, to see what it was like, and how he had best fight with it. After this he returned home, and at great trouble and expense had a dragon made out of wood, and covered it to look exactly like the real one. Then he taught his horse to gallop up to it without fear, and his two large dogs to fly at it, and how and where to do so, and when they were all well trained, he put on his armour, and taking his sword and spear he rode away. But, first of all, I should tell you, he prayed to God to guide him and give him victory. The other knights forgot that. Then watching the proper time when the dragon was full of food, and heavy and slow, he attacked him. The dogs flew at the living dragon just as they had learnt to fly at the wooden one, and worried and drew off his attention from the knight, who had only as yet blunted his spear point against the hard scales of the beast; but at length, as he reared himself up in great fury, he exposed a soft part of his body, when the knight instantly pierced him through and killed him. And so he ridded the poor people of that country of their great enemy.

Here, you see, this young knight, with only his dogs, was able to kill the giant, because in everything he went to work *in the right way*. You may be quite sure that where there's a will there is always a way, and a right way, to do good things.

But let me remind you of a much better story than this, because a *true* one. You have all read about David, who was only a boy, and yet slew the giant Philistine of Gath. You remember that king Saul lent him his armour to fight in, but that David " put it off," because he could not trust in it. He had never worn armour. He knew more about simpler things. He put his trust—that means his faith—in God, and taking only a sling and a stone, killed the giant in a moment! You don't know what strong armour this faith is in everything. The boy who says " I can't," depend upon it he never will ; but if he says " I will," and means it, you may be equally sure he can and will, *if he goes to work in the right way*.

Well, to go on about the Christian knights who determined to stop the cruelty I was telling you about. They knew at once they had lots of work to do, and a very difficult battle to fight.

Now I dare say you understand by this time what I mean by giants in these days. If they were Goliaths and dragons, we should have to kill them as *they* were killed; but the giants we are now talking about, as I showed you before, are of another sort. You know all about the Egyptian king, Pharoah, who made his servants so cruel to the Israelites. He was a very terrible giant, because he could do such a lot of mischief by making thousands of others as cruel as himself. Then, suppose, you had a bad heart that made you do cruel and wicked things, that heart would be *your* giant, and you would be its servant. So, you see, wicked people are their *own* giants!

Well, then, as these knights could not go killing giants in the old story fashion, they had to do it in the new fashion, and as they were wiser than the knights that fought with the dragon, they first of all did exactly what the *young* knight did. They took a look at the enemy, and they saw he was terribly strong— I mean that they found the giants and their servants were so many that they could not hope to fight them without a great deal of help. So I'll tell you what they did. They determined to get up a great army that should be greater than all the giants and their servants together, and to ask the nobles and other great people to join them. In a little time they did join them, and the king's ministers made a grand law against cruelty, just as they had done against slavery, and some time after that the Queen joined them also, and from that day they called this band of gentlemen the "Royal Society" for protecting these poor slaves.

Now, if you have not guessed already, as I daresay most of you have done, I had better tell you who these poor slaves were. Some people (and great people too) call them " Our *dumb companions;*" also "*Our four-footed friends;*" and many are called "*Our children's pets;*"—very good names too, but you will know them best as "*our dumb animals,*" and you will soon see how true all I have been telling you is.

Of course, you will think that what the Queen joined, everybody would join; but when you get older, you will see that good things grow very slowly, but bad, like weeds, very fast. So at first this "Society" was very small. Many people didn't care about it; others didn't understand it. They did not think that animals suffered pain! They thought that, as animals could not *speak*, they could not *feel*. But the good people said if they could not speak that was the very reason we should speak *for* them. The elephant, as you well know, is very strong, and the horse very swift, and the bullock very patient; and you know they do all sorts of work for us that we can't do for ourselves, and ought we not to do something for them that they can't do for *themselves?* But you see many of these thoughtless people I first spoke of never read their Bibles, and did not know that God had said,—" Thou shalt open thy mouth for the dumb." Many of these same people were very kind and merciful to other people, but they had not read another thing in the Bible—" The righteous man regardeth the life of his beast."

There is another thing still they had not read, but you will remember that our Saviour says if you only love those who love you, that you are no better than the common bad people, because they all do that! He says you must love those who don't love you, and do all you can for them; but these poor *animals will* love you if you are only kind to them, and their love is worth having, I can tell you. There are hundreds of pretty stories you may read to show you how they can love; how many wonderful and kind things they have done, and how many people's lives some of them have saved; but I can't remember more than one story of their hating, or taking revenge upon anybody. This was about an elephant that had a most cruel

Mahout, or driver. One day he was more brutally cruel to him than ever, when the poor animal, being perhaps nearly mad with pain and anger, seized the *Mahout* with his trunk, dragged him off his neck, put his foot upon him, and crushed him to death! This was a terrible punishment for cruelty; but now see what the elephant did next. The poor wife, seeing her husband killed, and being nearly mad with distress, hardly knowing what she did, took her child, and threw him before the elephant, saying—"There! you have killed my husband, take my son too!"—but instead of that, the elephant lifted up the little boy, and put him gently on his neck; meaning to show that he made him his driver in place of his cruel father!

Well, these knights and gentlemen I was telling you about, got officers, called "Agents," to go about and bring all the people they caught being cruel to animals before the Magistrate, who punished them as they deserved. So, kind-hearted people seeing all this being done to prevent cruelty, were greatly pleased, and many joined the Society, and gave loads of money to help it. Money you know is the only gunpowder—and the pen the only sword—and the tongue the only spear wanted for this kind of fighting. So in this way ladies can fight too, and some fight famously I can tell you—sometimes better than the knights! Many (both ladies and gentlemen) gave more than a thousand pounds at once—or more than ten thousand rupees; others gave 500, and 400, and 100 pounds, and hundreds of people gave smaller sums of money every year; so this "Royal Society" became at last very great. The Queen of England is at the head of it, and Dukes and Earls and Bishops and gentlemen of all kinds are happy to be its servants; and now a whole band of brave ladies have joined the Society, too, and are working and fighting as hard as they can in their own way.

Now, see what a capital thing good *example* is, for presently many other places all over England, Ireland, and Scotland began to get up Societies too, and then all the other countries in Europe did the same! So now there are nearly forty Societies in Great Britain; and in France, Germany, Italy, Austria, Russia, Switzerland, Holland, and Denmark, there are about one hundred! In America there are nearly a dozen more. There is one in Australia, and there are two in Africa! So you see what a grand army altogether there is now fighting against cruelty.

I have been telling you all this for two reasons: first, that you may think how much must be thought about mercy to animals when so many hundreds, as there are, of noblemen and gentlemen, who made these Societies, and have loads of other work and fighting to do, are willing and delighted to work and to fight for their poor dumb neighbours; and next that you may see how many giants of cruelty there must be in the world to *require* so many knights and gentlemen to be always fighting against them !— and you will understand what a sad load of cruel things must be done even in England, when I tell you that the "Royal Society" of London last year punished nearly 1,400 men for being cruel !

I have already told you some of the ways in which people are cruel to their dumb servants. I will tell you a few more to show you what these poor creatures have to suffer, and how much fighting there is yet to do for them. Some are made to drag heavy loads when the yoke or the saddle or collar is pressing upon a dreadful wound ; or when they are lame, very old and weak, and quite unfit to work, and are cruelly flogged to make them work ; and some are driven till they drop down dead, or are brutally beaten for not doing what they cannot do. Some that don't work for us, because too young, and can only die for us, are slowly bled to death, to make their flesh white meat. Fortunately the doctors now tell people this is not only very cruel to animals, but very bad for men too, and you will find that all cruelty is bad for us in some way. Some poor creatures are cut across the body whilst alive, to make them curl up! others, more horrible still, are boiled alive! and thousands of thousands are allowed to die slowly of suffocation, instead of being put to death quickly, and without more than a moment's pain, whilst many more thousands are skinned alive! Some have had their eyes put out to make them sing better! Many are taught to fight and wound each other with long steel spikes or spurs fastened to their legs; hundreds of beautiful birds are confined in cages and allowed to fly out suddenly only to let cruel people shoot at them,—to kill, wound, and mangle them, merely for the pleasure of shooting at a mark, when a wooden bird, or a target would do just as well. Other poor animals are let loose for gentlemen on horseback to run for miles after them, with dogs, that at last catch and bite and worry them to death.

Many more cruel things I might tell you about, but I think I have told you enough. Perhaps you'll be surprised when I tell you that many people, who, as I said before, are very kind to each other, don't see any cruelty in some of these things; and we must not be surprised or angry at this, because we understand the reason.

WHY PEOPLE ARE CRUEL.

They don't feel the pain themselves—the poor sufferers can't speak, and these otherwise kind people forget that they can *feel*, because they were never taught to think anything about it *when they were young;* and so they have *got accustomed to it.* This is just what happened with many very horrible things that used to be done a long time ago, when men and women were put to different dreadful kinds of death and torture too shocking to talk further about. People had *got accustomed to see it.* This is the reason why thousands of people do wrong in many other things besides cruelty, and why all of us, old and young, think so little of doing wrong in some way perhaps every day of our lives; it is because we have *got accustomed to it;* and so this is the reason we want you, now that you are young, *not* to get accustomed to cruelty, but to see it with all your eyes, and to hate it with all your hearts.

Now then I have told you how the knights and gentlemen of England and Scotland and Ireland got up what I have called a great army to fight against cruelty, and I have shown you how nearly all the other countries in the world afterwards did the same, and they have all been fighting very hard ever since, and have punished I don't know how many thousands of cruel people; but there is one country—one whole quarter of the globe I said nothing about—that is, ASIA. This you all know is where we are. Now, as Asia is bigger than Europe, and Europe has more than one hundred and forty "Societies,' how many do you think Asia ought to have ?— Asia has only *one*; and that is in Calcutta; so you see what a tremendous load of work there is to be done; and I can tell you that there are some cruelties done in India too horrible to describe to you,—and all because the people were not taught better *when they were young.*

Perhaps you ask why doesn't the great "Royal Society" in London (which we call our Parent Society) send some of its officers out here. Oh! they could not afford that! They have enough of fighting to do there, and every country must find its own army. They did all they could for us, as good parents always do. They showed us how to begin, and what to do, and gave us their Law, and told us all they had done, and now they expect us to do our best and fight for ourselves. Well, we have been fighting for eight years, and have had more than seven thousand cruel men punished in Calcutta. But these cruel and foolish people don't seem to care about a little punishment; so they get punished over and over again, and this is not what we have been fighting for. We don't want to be always punishing. We want to prevent cruelty, and punishing, too, if we can. These seven thousand foolish men have lost more than fourteen thousand rupees by being *fined!* and we would rather they should keep their rupees, and be kind to their dumb servants.

So, now we want to try another sort of fighting that ought in time to kill all the giants in the world! We want to get up a grand army here that shall be larger if possible than the whole army of cruel giants in India put together. Perhaps you know that in a real army there are different kinds of soldiers—horse soldiers, foot soldiers, and what are called Pioneers, or Sappers and Miners, who go before and prepare the way. Well, then, I'll tell you now what we want. We want plenty of *young Soldiers* to be our "Pioneers."—WE WANT YOU ALL TO JOIN US! We want you to be our Sappers and Miners!—"Oh!" (I think I hear you cry) "what can *I* do? I'm too young."—Not a bit! Remember the fable of the little mouse that released the great lion from his prison. He did with his little mouth what all the strength of the lion could not do with his powerful limbs. This is just what you can do, only you will use your tongues instead of your teeth! "Jack the Giant Killer," you know, was only a little boy, and he killed the giants, not by his strength, but his *wit*. He was very clever, but the giants were very stupid. And you will remember the *true* giant killer, David, who killed Goliath, not by his strength, but because God helped him. Now if you will only join us, I can promise that God will help *you*. You will very soon see in what way.

Let me just tell you how to begin. First of all you must be sure you never *do anything cruel yourselves!*—because many children do cruel things sometimes without knowing it! People, you know, can only be cruel to things smaller or weaker in some way than themselves. Just see how cowardly that is! So children can only be cruel to little animals, and we find them sometimes tormenting kittens and puppies and monkeys, throwing stones at frogs, robbing birds' nests, and killing beautiful butterflies and moths and beetles, and many other insects, only for amusement. Well, if ever you find yourselves going to do anything of this kind, and should remember those grand words—" Blessed are the merciful "—and *not* do it, you will have killed a giant at once, and God will have helped you! In this way perhaps you may kill a good many giants to begin with! Then when other boys and girls see that you won't do cruel things, they will begin to leave off doing them, too, because children don't care about amusements that others won't join in. They will get ashamed of doing what you won't do, and begin to think you are right; and so you may kill many more giants! Then, most of you can speak one of the native languages, and you can talk, as you do talk, a great deal, perhaps, to the servants, and can show how cruel some things are you may chance to see them do, and make them think more kindly about animals. When you see drivers of poor horses and bullocks cruelly beating or tormenting them in any way, you can speak kindly to such men, and tell them how wicked it is, and many men will think *much more* about what a child will say to them, and be more ashamed of being corrected *by you*, than if a grown up person scolded them. A kind word does not offend, but angry words sometimes do more harm than good; and so you will do what the young knight did with the dragon—find out their soft part—that is, *their heart*—and without wounding, you will in this way pierce it through, and kill a giant! Then, when these people leave off any cruel habits, *their children won't learn them*, because you know where there is no seed, there can be no tree. So, in this way you can be capital Sappers and Miners!

Then, again, you can persuade people not to suffocate their poor birds by shutting them up in cages covered with thick cloth, so that they never see the light, or get fresh air, which is done, as they tell you, to make them sing. I am sure you will think their singing must be their crying. Besides this, you can ask them to put their poor singing prisoners into larger cages, and give their parrots longer and lighter chains, and better perches, and be more careful of them. You will take care also never to let people, if you can prevent it, cruelly cut off your little dog's ears or tail, or spoil the beautiful tail of the beautiful horse by shortening it, and so taking from him the grand *chowree* which God gave him to keep off his tormentors—the flies and musquitoes!

Many more things than these you can do; but there is only one more I will mention now. Ask Papa or Mamma to subscribe for you to the "ANIMAL WORLD"—a large and charming book, began two years ago, full of delightful pictures, intended for young, and old, too. Say hat it will make a beautiful "*Christmas Box*" for you, and only cost two rupees a year to go on with, and so you will receive a new one every month. Or, if you have brothers or young friends, perhaps you can club together to buy it, and so have what is called a "*Book Club.*" If you will only read this book when you have it, you will get more and more in love with animals, and wish more and more to do them all the good you can. I have told you what a great thing *faith* is, and you will find that *example* is another, for in this way you will persuade loads of your young friends to "enlist"; and so we shall, by-and-bye, have such an army of young knights that in time all the giants of cruelty in India will be killed outright!

Now, then, I have only one more thing to say,—but it is a very great one. I have been talking to you about cruelty to Animals, and persuading you to join in being their friends; but you must not think that by this you will be doing good to *animals only*. Many people, who don't care about animals, say—"Oh, why don't you get up Societies to prevent cruelty to men."—This is exactly what I want to tell you that you *will* be doing by being *a friend to animals*. *Men* are animals, only God has made them very superior. He has given them wonderful minds and great knowledge, and so in hundreds of ways they can take care of themselves, as common animals cannot do.

Then one man can only be cruel to another when he is stronger, and has a bad heart, and has got so *accustomed* to see and to do cruel things, that he does not know he *is* doing cruel things, and does not think anything at all about it. Thousands of people are cruel to animals, because, as I said before, they have got accustomed to it, not because they love cruelty, but from *want of thought*,—and this is because they were never taught, *when young*, what things *are* cruel.

Now, what I want you to remember is this—that the child who is cruel to *an animal*, when he gets older *will be cruel to men*. Ask Papa and Mamma if I am not right; and so if you are accustomed to be very kind to animals, you will learn to be kind to every living creature, and this is the true way to be kind to yourselves. People who are selfish and ignorant, too, and think only about themselves and their own pleasures, find at last that other people don't care about *them*. Many are cruel to animals from *ignorance*, and find out, afterwards, that they have been cruel *to themselves, too*. I could tell you hundreds of ways in which they do this. I will tell you only one. People in England and other countries used to shoot all the poor small birds they found. Some did this for amusement, and others because they thought the birds spoilt a little of their corn and other plants; but they have found out their mistake. When the birds were killed, the insects, *that the birds used to feed upon*, grew into millions that did indeed spoil and eat up the plants! So the farmers found they had been killing their best friends; and now they won't allow the little birds to be killed in their fields at all! So, you see that God intended that these little creatures should be happy, too; that they should do us good, and *not* harm.

Now, I hope you all intend to "enlist" to make up this grand army we want to fight against cruelty: and that you will all turn out brave young Knights and Ladies,—never afraid to defend the weak, or to speak for those that *cannot speak for themselves*. Remember the golden rule given us in the Bible, to "do to others as you would that they should do to you," and depend upon it that the real way to be happy yourselves is to make *others* happy, and so you will find that real pleasure is *in doing good*.

HYMN.

...ressly for the Children of the Sunday Schools of
Calcutta:

...ames Gregor Grant, Esq., Durham.

God of ceaseless loving kindness!
   Guide us, lest we quit Thy way,
From the mists of sinful blindness
   Purge and free us, Lord, we pray!

Let our spirits, meek and grateful,
   Strive to know, and feel and see
Cruel thoughts and deeds are hateful
   Evermore, O Lord to Thee!

Thou to erring man hast given
   O'er Thy humbler creatures power—
See! o'er-loaded and o'er-driven,
   They are tortured hour by hour!

Yet—o'er-loading, and o'er-driving,
   Day by day, the long year through,
Tyrant *man* himself is striving
   Less to bear, and less to do!

Oft he murmurs "*master urgeth
Tasks beyond the worst slave's share!*"
Yet his own dumb beast he scourgeth
   Till the stricken bones are bare!

LORD! the meanest thing that crawleth
   Still THY loving care enfolds!
Still to ground no sparrow falleth
   But THY loving eye beholds.

Teach us then, in field or city,
   On the shore, or on the sea,
God of Mercy, Love, and Pity!
   Kind to all thy works to be!

On fair lands, or shores the bleakest,
   Wheresoever their lot may fall,
Largest, smallest, strongest, weakest,
   THOU hast made and loved them all!

Then with spirits meek and grateful,
   Make us strive to feel and see
Cruel acts to Beasts are hateful
   Evermore, O Lord to THEE!

CALCUTTA SOCIETY FOR PREVENTION OF CRUELTY TO ANIMALS.

PATRON:

His Excellency the Right Hon'ble the Earl of Mayo, Viceroy and Governor General.

PRESIDENT:

The Venerable Archdeacon Pratt, M.A.

COMMITTE.

- APCAR, T. A., ESQ.
- BARRY, DR. J. B.
- BLECHYNDEN, A. H., ESQ.
- BRUCE, J. S., ESQ.
- CHAPMAN, R. B., ESQ., C.S.
- CHEVERS, NORMAN, ESQ., M.D.
- CRAWFORD, J. A., ESQ., C.S.
- DAVIS, W. P., ESQ.
- DON, THE REV. J. D.
- HOGG, STUART, ESQ., C.S.
- HEERA LAL SEAL, BABOO.
- KUMAR HARENDRA KRISHNA RAI BAHADOOR.
- LONG, THE REV. J.
- MONCRIEFF, R. S., ESQ.
- MOONSHEE UMEER ULLEE, KHAN BHADOOR.
- MOULVIE UBDOOL LUTEEF, KHAN BAHADOOR.
- PEARY CHAND MITTRA, BABOO.
- ROBERTSON, J. L., ESQ.
- RUSTOMJEE, MANUCKJEE, ESQ.
- SMITH, ALEX, ESQ., C.S.
- SMITH, D. A., ESQ.
- TURNBULL, COLONEL, MONTAGUE J.

OBJECTS OF THE SOCIETY.—To prevent the cruel and improper treatment of animals, and ameliorate their condition generally throughout India; and secondarily—To exercise educational influence in cultivating merciful impulses and humanity towards man.

ITS PLANS ARE PRINCIPALLY—

1. The Agency of paid European officers to watch, warn, and prosecute all persons found guilty of cruelty to animals,

2. The distribution of printed papers in the various languages of India, conveying instruction and warning.

3. The introduction into Schools and elsewhere of Books, or Tracts, in English and the vernacular, "calculated to impress on youth the duty of humanity towards the inferior animals."

4. Seeking the aid of the Pulpit, the Press, and all Public Instructors, in advocating the principles and objects of the Society.

Communications and Contributions will be thankfully received by the Secretary on behalf of the Committee.

COLESWORTHEY GRANT,
Hony. Secretary and Treasurer.

2, *Mission Row, Calcutta,* 1871.

PRINTED BY THACKER, SPINK, & CO., CALCUTTA.

Printed by Libri Plureos GmbH in Hamburg,
Germany